to miss caichey

Thank you for seatty

Facts About the Three Toed Sloth

By Lisa Strattin

© 2016 Lisa Strattin

How to caise a two toed sloth,

Love giselle p.

Facts for Kids Picture Books by Lisa Strattin

Canada Lynx, Vol 114

Blue Tarantula, Vol 115

Giant Tarantula, Vol 116

Common Nighthawk, Vol 117

Nile Crocodile, Vol 118

Nilgai, Vol 119

North American Porcupine, Vol 120

Numbat, Vol 121

Nuthatch, Vol 122

Nyala, Vol 123

Sign Up for New Release Emails Here

http://lisastrattin.com/subscribe-here

Join the KidCrafts Monthly Program Here

http://KidCraftsByLisa.com

Table of Contents

INTRODUCTION

Sloths are the slowest moving mammal in the world. They can climb only 8 feet every minute and, in fact, move so slowly that algae and moths live in their fur. Although it's named the three-toed sloth, their toes don't move like yours or mine do. Rather, they are locked in place and are hidden under their fur. What we see as toes are actually long, curved claws, which the sloth can use to hang from trees and branches.

There are four species—or kinds—of three-toed sloth; the brown-throated, the pale-throated, the maned, and the pygmy. All of them live in the dense forests of South America.

CHARACTERISTICS

When seen sitting upright—as they might be in zoos—their fur looks strange and puffy. This is because a sloth's fur grows to hang upside down—which is how they spend much of their time when hanging from branches. Sloths spend nearly their entire lives in the tops of trees—it's where they eat, and even where they sleep.

Sloths only use the bathroom about once a week! When they do, they leave their treetop homes and descend to the forest floor. There, not only do they relieve themselves, but they also come into contact with the algae, fungus, and moths that live in their fur.

While sloths are strong climbers, they are very bad at walking on land. Their long claws get in the way of crawling, and their hind legs are almost useless. To walk, they have to dig their front claws into the ground and pull their body and back legs along—almost as if they were climbing up a tree trunk. Exposed in this way, they are defenseless against leopards and other large predators. Perhaps uniquely among mammals, sloth can't regulate their own body temperature. Instead, they rely on the sun to keep them warm, much in the same way that reptiles and amphibians do.

APPEARANCE

A sloth's fur is brown and gray, and the algae that lives on them gives them a green tint that acts like camouflage in the trees. They have long legs but short bodies, and three-toed sloths have short, thick tails.

Three-toed sloths have nine bones in their neck, which is quite unusual among mammals. People have only seven bones in their neck—and so do giraffes, whose necks can be up to six-feet long!

The extra bones in a sloth's neck allow them to rotate their heads almost completely around, much like an owl's! This extra movement lets the sloth to see what's going on around him, without forcing him to move his extraordinarily slow body.

LIFE STAGES

A mother three-toed sloth is pregnant for around six months—though other kinds of sloth have longer pregnancies. After they're born, baby sloths will cling to their mother's coat for more than a month, and even when they are able to climb on their own, they stay near their mother for as many as four years. Depending on the species, they are considered mature at between three and five years.

For the first nine months or so of a baby's life, the mother will stay in the same tree, eating the tree's leaves and feeding the baby milk. As the baby becomes older and more independent, however, the mother will broaden her range, moving from tree to tree and leaving the baby for longer and longer periods until the baby is grown.

Adult sloths are solitary animals, and prefer to live alone. Often, a sloth will prefer to eat the leaves of a particular kind of tree, and its territory will be all of that kind of tree in a particular area. This behavior allows two or more sloths to live very near each other, without fighting each other over food.

LIFE SPAN

Sloths can live for as long as 30 years.

SIZE

About the size of a small dog, three-toed sloths are between one-and-a-half and two-and-a-half feet long, and weigh between 10 and 17 pounds.

17

HABITAT

Three-toed sloths live exclusively in South America, primarily in dense jungles and rain forests. They spend most of their lives at the tops of trees, only coming down to move from one tree to another (or to use the bathroom!).

Unlike their shorter-limbed, two-clawed cousins, three-toed sloths are actually pretty good swimmers, and will often drop from high in a tree to splash land into a river. Their long, powerful arms give them strong swimming strokes, and in this way they sometimes move from tree to tree more safely than if they have to crawl on land.

DIET

Living as they do at the tops of trees, sloths eat leaves. However, the leaves they eat don't give them much energy—which helps explain why they move so slowly.

The leaves of rainforest trees are also often full of chemicals that most animals can't eat. To get around this, the sloth has evolved a stomach that has four parts. Each of these parts is home to many different kinds of bacteria, which allows the sloth to digest the trees' toxic leaves.

Because of this multi-chambered stomach, it takes between two and four weeks for a sloth to digest a single meal— which explains its peculiar bathroom habits!

FRIENDS AND ENEMIES

Sloths have some strange friends. Its fur is dense and course, which allows for the algae and fungi, that it comes into contact with on the forest floor, to grow. This gives the algae and fungus a safe place to live, and gives the sloth the green camouflage it needs to hide from predators.

Along with algae and fungus, a sloth's fur also houses moths—which both find the sloth to be a safe place to live, and also provide fertilizer for the algae. What the moths gain from this relationship is access to what the sloth leaves on the forest floor every week, in which the moths will lay their eggs.

A sloth's enemies include the rainforest's top predators—big cats like leopards, large snakes, and some of the larger birds like owls and eagles.

SUITABILITY AS PETS

While the big-eyed, slow moving animals may seem to make good pets, they would actually be pretty difficult to take good care of. This is because they have specialized diets, and require lots and lots of fresh, hard-to-find leaves in order to stay healthy. Not only that, but the algae that grows in their fur actually helps provide them with nutrients—and this alga wouldn't grow well inside a person's home.

Nevertheless, they aren't dangerous animals and, in zoos, keepers are able to handle them with relative ease, often letting them hang from their backs and shoulders while they give demonstrations.

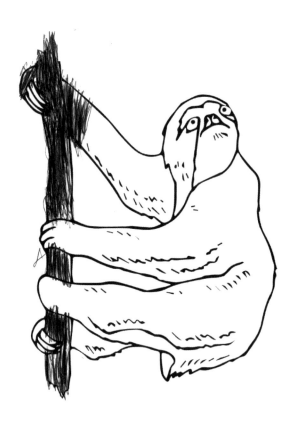

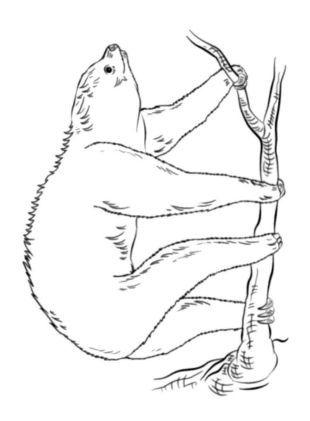

Please leave a review for me

http://lisastrattin.com/Review-Vol-129

For more Kindle Downloads Visit Lisa Strattin Author Page on Amazon Author Central

http://amazon.com/author/lisastrattin

To see upcoming titles, visit my website at LisaStrattin.com – all books available on kindle!

http://lisastrattin.com

PLUSH THREE TOED SLOTH

You can get one by copying and pasting this link
into your browser:

http://lisastrattin.com/plushsloth

KIDCRAFTS MONTHLY
SUBSCRIPTION PROGRAM

Receive a Box of Crafts and a Lisa Strattin Full Color Paperback Book Each Month in Your Mailbox!

Get yours by copying and pasting this link into your browser

http://kidcraftsbylisa.com

Printed in Great Britain
by Amazon